The Uniform House

Acknowledgments

Grateful acknowledgement is made to the following publications, where certain of these poems have previously appeared: *Birmingham Poetry Review*: "Ancient, Immaterial"; "Grant in the Valleys" and "In the Republic of Tinnitus"; *Concho River Review*: "Recitation of the Pepper Cure"; *The Georgetown Review*: "Calamity's Blacktops"; *The Greensboro Review:* "Sun Stylus, Montgomery"; *Gulf Coast:* "Autumn Techne" and "This Paradise Valley—A Blues for Robert Hayden"; *Hubbub*: "Rayon is Probably the Most Misunderstood of All Fibers"; *The Louisville Review:* "Fluorescent Blues"; *New South*: "The Uniform House of Dixie" and "Versus Physiognomy's Prophets"; *Sewanee Theological Review:* "The Painted Men"; *Southern Humanities Review:* "Country of Stopped Clocks"; *The Sow's Ear Poetry Review:* "N.O. Prescription"; *Steel Toe Review:* "A Cutting," "In Loco Parentis" and "Tools and Utilities"; *TriQuarterly*: "Music at the Furnaces"; *Valparaiso Poetry Review*: "Basement Occupations"; *Waccamaw*: "Joy Spring Diamond"; *West Branch*: "Through the Chagall Windows"; *Whatever Remembers Us: An Anthology of Alabama Poetry*: "Almost Georgic, Alabama"

Special thanks to Juan Carlos Galeano, to Lesley Jenike, to Alan Shapiro, to Hena Skelton, to Scott Stephens, to Sue Brannan Walker and to Greg Williamson.

Also in memory of Jake Adam York, dear friend and fellow traveler (1972-2012)

The Uniform House

A Negative Capability Press Book

Published in the United States of America by
Negative Capability Press
62 Ridgelawn Dr. East
Mobile, AL 36608

Production and design by HTDesignS

Printed in the United States of America

Copyright © 2014 by James L. Murphy
ISBN 978942544930
LCCN 2014936447

Scan to visit
www.negativecapabilitypress.org

Scan to visit and like
Negative Capability on Facebook

In Memory of my Father,
John Charles Murphy (1932-2012)

CONTENTS

II

"O ben finiti, o già spiriti eletti,"
Virgilo incominciò, "per quella pace
ch'i' credo che per voi tutti s'aspetti,

ditene dove la montagna giace,
sì che possibil sia l'andare in suso;
chè perder tempo a chi più sa più spiace."

"Oh you who ended well," Virgil began,
"oh spirits already chosen, by that peace
which I believe awaits you every one,

tell us in what place the mountain slopes
so that it would be possible to climb,
for who knows most grieves most at the loss of time."

—Dante, *Purgatorio, Canto III*
(Trans. W.S. Merwin)

I

The Uniform House of Dixie

Plangent notes of the nineteen thirties —
rattletraps listing over improvised bricks,
streaks of silver down the tracks, threads

greening in the back lot behind Sammy's
Our Place Cafeteria. In little summer
variations keening, skipping off the frets —

the revolution ushered in by Charlie
Christian hanging there for all to hear.
A cantilevered ladder team applies

broad strokes to the vacant building,
rolling dream insignias into brusque reality —
A full range of quality apparel for policemen,

military, doctors, nurses, dairy men, boy scouts,
bus drivers, prisoners, drug store, football,
Pullman porter, dentist's office, sanitation, every need —

First Try the Uniform House of Dixie —
two paint-decked men mixing every shade
thirty feet above the buzzing avenue.

Haze of progress settles on the carriage —
hip-swung hems and black-lined calves
drawing off-color jokes and hoots — the usual

crowd pushes on its blind particulate way.
Here's a woman's gaze caught in a compact
mirror. Here's the sudden stripping of a glove,

ringed finger in the corner of a half-closed eye.

The atmosphere's a smokehouse tinged
with oily creosote. Old ailments that defy

all economics traverse pipes and flanges
underground far out as Bessemer. And all this
involves the way palms shine mute brass

handles of the trolley cars, the fall of lines
for county-wide elections, someone's
carefully engineered education in decay,

tips and keys to the downtown mission.
Still someone gets the message — unspoken,
sudden as a cloudburst in a stenciled sky —

notes that patter in frissons of individuated
nightmare and elation — one and all together.
Birmingham Business Looks to the Forties

ducks cleaned and pressed, shoes cork-soled,
crisp and stepping to, in line, seams tight,
eyes front, and ready for the coming wars.

This Paradise Valley: A Blues for Robert Hayden

Three ages of a life are nailed into
my wall—corpse cleaving into soldier,
soldier into infant—an inverted calyx
you would have recognized at once.

As it is, I have Memphis Slim in a three-inch
speaker and the nightsongs of Alabama
to comfort and conduct me past the trellis
to some place where you are—distant

as the pharaohs, now—quiet as this midnight
fog that wraps the long-needle pines in their enduring
mystery. It's a claustrophobic space—always
too hot—the box we're sealed in—blind

as night itself. The ink flows as from
a wound to you. Our weary language buckles—
I speak American, like you, drink long
drafts of fake beliefs, sweet for that old jelly-roll,

what can I do? Double-back in history,
stake some claim that shifts and grows up
wrong before my eyes. My daughter on
the ethernet might one day abide we

confused fools of the United States—
Paradise seekers, crumblers, singers taking stock.
When she comes to you I hope she's wide
awake, so your songs can drum the nation home.

Music at the Furnaces

For every Pentecostal child led by the hand, spun around in front of the stark chromatic Thunderbird and forced to watch the glowing cataract in terror *so you can see what hell looks like* —

For every spidery guitarist or hot piano strider direct from Anniston, Alabama who later failed to reach Chicago, buried under heaps of the "Coal Mountain Blues"
(Sonny Scott and Walter Roland, *c.* 1933) —

For James Withers Sloss, Daniel Pratt, and the other boutoniered barons who crossed roads in the Jones Valley, threw up the shotgun houses, and trained the produce of the old New South straight from Birmingham and Bessemer to every navy yard
on earth —

this ghoulish amplification of a harp, distorted voice, these undead drums and bass now jack-knifing against the rust-flaked walls, between the stacks and long-cold furnaces, among these crumbling brick aortas plugged with coke.

Some blues gone, some to begin. A polite summer crowd in from a light rain learns just how the country comes to town — shakily, in a drunken shambles, stumbling up to speak on history. *That wasn't no plaything. When you got in the gate everything's dangerous — overhead, underhead, dangerous, you know.*

Some mighty thunderclap far off in the county now reaffirms this truth. It's my job to chuckle — my self a man whose single visible scar is the result of never learning how to properly iron a cotton shirt. I was so unschooled, I couldn't stay on the cool side of the iron.

Someone counts time, and a prehistoric chord progression binds us all together. We're on the watch for whatever satan each one knows, along with every glassy turquoise, green or yellow eye of slag that stares up from the ground.

One October Clearing

Gathered, prodded, doused, then lit afire —
       little death's head at the center of the leaf-pile
              grins and glows — consuming summer's

last vestiges — crackle of a baseball season,
       beach vacation, birthday party — all risen
              into the breath-clear afternoon.

And in the tinctured air, that blue-gray fascination —
       dust of wings and playground metal,
              efflux of cold creeks, smokestacks, diesel,

rumble of the trains — boxcars that cube the sunlight —
       Red Wings and Wells-Lamont, blackwatch
              plaid on quilted flannel, rakes and thatchers,

bluejays, pinecones, and all the smoking cylinders.
       This is my father's territory. None of it is mine,
              though I play here at its margins,

always watching other people work. The coaling
       waste wood crumbles, the oak leaves
              erupt and something frees itself at once —

a filament is snapped, a trace is lost, a synapse
       burns apart. And in the clear space, simple
              temperature, cooling into coming fall.

Joy Spring Diamond

A pretty signature three lines above my own —
so the leatherbound registry forces many years
down through the bone-broad curvatures

where every name is made. "Joy Spring" —
the ever black and white jazz standard rose,
always buoyant, wing-tip tapping, exhalant

mother-bloom — and "Diamond" — edge of
transubstantiated light—a hard old needle
digging in this porous earth for harmonies.

Was she born in a spongy shuttered house,
tongues of lead on every peeling surface?
Or in some communal manger, half choked

by desperate spirits of the healed and saved?
In a cloud white limo? At the movies?
Where is she at this moment? Sublimely

gliding through the shattered bricks of 1963,
peering up close at an opaque minstrel show,
kneeling suddenly to cross herself between

apalling torchlight and a trumped-up charge —
torn down — now right here in the present, safe
behind the velvet ropes and temporary chains.

Only one figure at the cumulus bay window's
counting in the instant when my writing hand
just stops for the small prayer of her name.

Autumn Techne

On command, a thousand dogs explode
from the banks of manmade lakes,

tails whipping on fat swells of water,
muzzles off, chokers thrown aside.

Then the masters' muted dialogue begins
as the formations of perforated birds

fall to every rippling surface. Two thousand
years of breeding, so the canine jaws

lock tight around each carcass — the kills
secure as dollars in a wallet. This way,

dawn light's tinted with blue smoke —
gold sunglasses, shotguns and cigars.

That way, each wild animal's on its haunches,
frozen deeper down the starvation chain.

We've burned gas, kerosene, loose tobacco,
whiskey, cooking oil, and above all, cash,

just in order to arrive. A drawn-out process
of *aficion* replaces wilderness with a formal thing

that shoots sparks, fells branches, takes
hulking steps and churns up brackish water,

gets drunk, paints its face, speculates
on weather and the land, dons rain gear, debates

forces driving this economy, then finds its own
natural catastrophe mandated by machine.

Vessels

(after a print by Scott Stephens)

A natural riot, the living record of every little
aspiration that rises as a tendril from the giving
ground into uncertain air — each one a prayer

for rain that has been answered — the sway
that in time textures the soil, feeds the leaves,
tears down the barbed wire fences, and solves

every human problem built onto the landscape —
you blindly work the body's medium, unite
the broken past to present and the sturdy dark

to light. You transform the hidden, flaccid joke
between the legs of every man into something
almost hopeful, if yet lacking manners. That's not

your fault. In a new mother, your blue tracks
travel the slopes of her full breasts, as you tend
to supply and demand. And you conduct

the mission, the milk, the miracle itself from
her body to the child's, where you're also
quietly at work, tapping your quick and fragile

message at the temples — *this can't wait, this can't
wait* — the same thing you always say, whether
it's water, blood, or wine that moves within you

to some better place beyond. Shear you and a great
oak topples. Slow you and my memory is choked,
my speech is twisted, my eyes go red and riverine.

I want to sing your praises now, drink you deeply,
admire your easy facility and rightly receive it,
because one day your faithful service will expire.

And then one of you will burst beneath my bones
and kill me. Will it be you, beautiful and vulnerable
protester? You, the one curled closest to my heart?

Sun Stylus, Montgomery

The star is a signatory—every numbered leaf
a small blind contract—only for this afternoon

overfilled with water, this one day stretched into
a complete summer, showing steady progress

as so much fine organic compost hurtles down—
finished blooms, rotten buds, sugar-heavy fruits,

the unbound leaves themselves, and now at last
a core-dead branch or two. This is the future time

I dreamed in Kansas, sight reduced to nothing
before the installation sculptures of the plains—

one solid Methodist red barn, a single piebald horse,
then the necessary stand of winded cottonwoods.

A different anger in the heat, another balled-up
darkness just outside the opaque basement windows

here in the temperate zone. How will I remember just
this play of clouds, this fugue of drunken honeysuckle,

the barometric pressure's hand against my chest?
Who will write the poem of this stormy Monday,

already made a monument on wax, and in streams across
black granite? The cover lifts and then surprise rays

snake across the gardens—cutting, shooting, scrawling
instruments—the laced fire of all stretched above-

ground life, infused in every volatile red rose, and in
gold bursts of jonquils. Another day handwritten

in some lost language—mediated—a rife, rifled,
ripe, ripped page burning in the southern sun.

Tools and Utilities

Solar power of a ninety degree Saturday —
the Chevron station's icy island, wrapped
in 808 bass beats, electric kudzu creeping

across the county road toward wilderness
while all here work their idle business — buying
milk or eggs, topping off the anti-freeze, going

in for cheap sunglasses, processed cheese food,
long fluorescent sugar bottles, fried chicken
dried to jerky under unrelenting lamps, every fast

grab item necessary to propel a sunburnt body
through the few prized minutes of a broiling
afternoon. I've run the squeegee notes over

my truck's windshield, and tried to rub away
the bug juice left behind. I've caught a Spanish
joke and laughter from the other pump,

good music for this market scene, almost
cheered enough to whistle up a tuneless happy
trill for Saturdays, and summer indolence,

when the white pickup — *Officer, that's right,
a white pickup* — cruises into place beside us.
It might have been a city cast-off, corrosive

fingers of rust fanning out from every dimple
in the body, bald tires, vast bed empty but for
two chubby twelve year-olds in string bikinis.

Two men up in the cab — one skinny seed hat
guy with chin fuzz trouble, one slumping, thirty-
five or so, crow's feet, rough hands, working.

The girls bounce up out of the box and hit
the asphalt, flip-flops and gaudy laughter —
too much dizzy laughter, and every man-jack

in the parking lot shifts his attention. The men
creak from the front of the truck — *No sir,*
I didn't hear or see anything especially suspicious, but —

they breeze into the food mart, straight up
to the tallboy tubs, while the girls pinwheel
around parked cars, pulling goofy faces at them

from the other side. It's in the legs and arms,
no one can deny it — *just kinda funny* — in an instant
what had drawn us to it now explodes in raw

alarm when fully recognized, all the slack gone
tight and dry, eyes strained behind dark glasses,
trying to peer over the misplaced neon strings

to see inside the blood — *Is everything ok? Ok?*
tap-tap — *the hell it is.* Six or seven seconds more,
the men return with big sacks full of beer,

perfect stuff for afternoons like these, the full
assorted colds of carbonation, thin hint of hops,
sweet rice, the chunks of clean company ice,

things most gathered here know very well.
They boost the girls back to their shaky places,
where they kick the empty toolbox, so that

it resonates like a tin gong made in shop class —
both flat and hollow, nonmusical, not a cymbal,
but a plate. Then with a little herky-jerky

left turn and a squeak of treads, they're gone.
What dark hand had passed over for a second,

snapped its fingers, and vanished in a cartoon

cloud? What explains the epidural chill that
fathered fear in me and in the others, just for
one moment, then was dismissed in a snap

choice to stay put, to tend our own timbers
before the specks of others — good judges,
moved and hardly certain, lazy and alive.

N.O. Prescription

She teases verses from a plastic box,
turns the dial to plenitude. One child cries,

one smears chocolate on the heirloom rug.
The singer offers her another bruising

round of soft condolence through the air.
A bright collapse of metal in the street—

daughter, dog, and husband rush at once
to see—sticky baby's fingering her hair.

This sleepy poltergeist now drops her mug
while she feels the droning licks unravel—

Well you know I'm not a doctor, darlin'—
but did you know I'm not a doctor's son?

A bottlefly lights on the marbled edge,
spins and tongues some crust of sugar.

Someone's always fallen from a limpid sky
at the treble end of this tradition.

Cross-hatched muscle memory drives
her fingers through this fretwork, daily

chrome fixtures flow, the batter thickens,
somehow her book gets written.

No sleep for days while her stories grow
from the sink to enormous proportions—

consciousness the sudden drug that cuts her
free as it uncurls, and drives these blues away.

Almost Georgic, Alabama

A young sorrel horse runs the fenceline,
great cords of muscle gather and release

floods of energy and acid — blood's light
clarified, its soul grown huge with speed.

Earth-red, set just above the shock-green
rolling pasture, momentary *Spiritus Mundi* —

the close and symbiotic presence bends
my dog's small will and mine from exercise.

Destinations fused for a few tight seconds,
five thousand years' geometry draws each

figure to the others — blink, step, breath —
to own and never know—to sprint in track

shoes, pant at the end of a leash, or graze
a barrier of metal tubes — in a flash of turf

and sunlight these natures practically collide,
each sure of its exact position and capacity.

To puzzle, to hunt, to flee — shared survival
strategies, homologous as bones and teeth.

I'm advised by horse and pointer, lectured
by insects, corrected by heat waves rippling

in the road's gray grip — what I had believed
part of the earth is atmosphere, as a flock

takes its tree aloft for one long moment
after the shotgun. A technique to cultivate

the spirit — turn the earth twice over, try to
learn all lore of the domestic. Failing this,

in late husbandry of the land, use muscle
memory, and, when thinned or broken,

the tracery each beat and breath provides.

Learning Norah's Stars

On her Baptism, 3 August 2008

Open to the world at first light,
she finds always a cool breeze
blows her way, and gentle music
plays in our two breaths beside
her. We awaken to the sparks
of smiles, the sudden gleam in
eyes that see and understand us,
even though she doesn't speak
in tones our jaded, full-grown
minds can start to contemplate
in English. And what she says,
in coos and squeals, in giggled
long and flamboyant sentences,
must be from another world—
pure Logos, direct and truthful
as dictation of the Stars. We
speak a slow *Good-Morning*,
reach for her toys and clothes,
and she startles, bubbles, flashes
an amazed grin, as if a birthday
cake arrived from behind the door.
Today, in our joy and jealousy,
Norah, we welcome you with Words,
with Water, and with constellated
blessings passed from hand to hand.
We've pledged to be your guides,
to teach you chart and sextant,

to help you as you navigate
the waves that crash our world.
But you, like all born on this earth,
began by breathing in the water.
How can our words go beyond
your lessons? Teach us how
to speak and listen simply,
close as you are to the stars.

In a Church of Epiphytes

The entire congregation of the tree assumes
a look of swaybacked weariness, more than

ancient, as the gray-green flames consume
the stock of metaphors surrounding it —

to draw life solely from blue sky and sunlight,
and steep carbon dioxide into the different

figures of oxygen, replenished and released
in the slow cool of June mornings — this is

God walking in the Garden. The little liars
run up the trunks. They listen for the symphony

to stop, sniff for far-off winter. But no one
ever comes to skin them. In each grove

the scene repeats, and as fat shadows shrink
to make plain the day's intentions, a million

testifying voices sing, suspended in mid-air.

Recitation of the Pepper Cure

The mouth is a small shrine where they hold sway —
serrano, tabasco, Scotch bonnet, habañero —
zealous paladins, the four horsemen of capsaicin —
midday cracked earth of the desert, night on the savannah —
little jaguar eyes, teeming jungle after rain —
the highest tree, the deepest canyon, the snaking Amazon —
summer asphalt spreader, nail factory, the devil's express train —
all human scales fall short as the Scoville units rise.
Take one to purify the palate, two to palliate the mind.

In Loco Parentis

But nothing works quite as it should —
large fistfuls of Bazooka gum, Pixie Stix,
mystery rings and bubba teeth, all pulled
from a huge hill of little plastic globes,
then even drippy patriotic bomb pops,
while we slosh our drive-up Daiquiris.
Everyone flashes cherry smiles, sugars
shining in our veins. No one speaks
at a decent volume. We've run the dog
from his narrow territory to feebly shake
behind a shrub, in absolute submission,
an elastic chaos bouncing all around him.
Has the harried cat committed suicide?
Have the egg-faced neighbors called
the cops? Are the bookshelves burning?
Will the handbrake hold? Is there pee
in the exotic garden fishpond? It seems
that one exhausted couple can be traded
for another — and this is living proof
that even the most fortunate arrangements
might hide unexpected funnies — God's
great gifts like stink loads in the atomizer,
bright chicklets of habañero pepper gum,
rubber snakes under the covers, whoopee
cushions set in church — all the good things
better angels may somehow yet deliver us.
Yet, caught in the silly present, my left knee
tightens like a packed snowball; my Cool

Joe shirt's been torn; the charcoal aviator
shades have slipped from my face; I blink
in and out like some rousted marsupial
and drag like a daysleeping ape. One boy
runs through tomato vines, cutting heads
with a pine branch sword, while his brother
creeps toward a screen door with the hose.
My ex-wife shakes her head and laughs at me.
Give it time, she says. *Just wait. All in good time.*

Stranger, Field and Horse

It's all about the roan I see slap sideways
on the turf — *She'll die — Must be dead already —*
What city boys remember from the picture
books and zoo farm trips is this sort of country
corn, so I swerve onto the gravel road, stop dead,
and power down my window. What am I going
to do now? Call the horse coroner from here?

Motionless in the longing daylight, flat face
planted in the muck — *How many hearts does
a horse have anyway? Are those legs cartilage
or bone?* She won't move an inch, stone dead
under my dumbfounded stare. Should I take
a picture or whistle loud across this wind, just
to see if she's really galloped up to horse heaven,

or wherever it is they go? I don't know the code,
the ruddy farmer or his lovely taken wife. I don't
know the crops, the straight life lines, the process
of a spring or fall, the raw milk or the mousers
that would tear my housecats' faces off for play
and leave them for the opossums. I do know
it's some crazy impulse that has drawn me out

into the cold air without a coat, heart sore for this
poor horse. It's the same sentimental box trap
that used to take my dollars for "Streets of Baltimore"
and billiards in long barlight afternoons. And still
I can't come home. I know I'm not the matter here,
and I'm about to go. That's when the dead horse
flicks her head and whispers *Fool, give it a rest.*

There's no one here but us. And I ain't talking.

Basement Occupations

Charred coffee zipped and sizzled
on the burner as a greasy ungloved hand
removed the pot then sloshed more
fingers of fuming tar into the cup.

A lip smack, indifferent sigh and a single
cloudy bead of sweat dropped straight off
the nose — it could be an interrogation
chamber, raked with hundred-watt bare light.

That array of pungent household poisons —
the chipped and dented cellar cabinets
holding jars of solvents, cans of reeking
pigments, paints, and tubs of cracking glue,

plus the t-shirts dipped in gasoline,
a row of cobwebbed empty wine jugs —
the raw materials of a tranquil revolution
staged against the sunlit workday world.

All day long the clank and rip of tools
that bent, smoothed, or sliced some unwilling
medium — cheap plywood to blinding chrome —
what did it matter? Whoever walked

into those tight, hot rooms to question why
was cursed — or even worse — informed.
Somewhere between daydream and idea,
play and plan, lived all this aimless industry.

Can you see him finally emerging from
whatever corner was his shop? That tattered,
years-old underwear, a vivid forearm tan,
red face flecked with motor oil, worn

shoes held off to one side and bare feet
on the tiles — then every son's bored groan
at his familiar, and every father's telling
nod or smile — *Someday, my boy, it's yours.*

Soul and Cinders

It's December, 1976 — my face bitten
by a blue Chicago gale, an annunciation

on every downturned corner of what life's
blood's pooling out around us. Treacherous

West Side legends enforce their codes
of brotherhood — barber pole, butcher

shop, billiard room, Cash 'n' Go. No telling
who I am aboard the train. Dad points

to chimneys smoking up the vista — the whole
wide horizon viewed from State and Lake

a dry ice factory, a blue pinwheel, a crystal rose
with airborne cancers lengthening the light.

*

Rolled onto the elevated plywood —

MARVIN GAYE LIVE IN CONCERT
M RVIN GA LIV IN CON ERT
MAR IN AYE IVE N ONCERT
 ARV N AY LI E IN CON ER
M RVI G Y LIV I CO E T

EZ-LOVE now scrawled cross his face
black horns, cigar and groucho glasses.

*

Thick music forced into transistor radios,
distorted so the cymbals fizz and bass licks

pop apart — *You don't have to worry that it's wrong.*
Voice just caught beneath the screaming brakes.

An obligatory iceball blows across the plexiglas
above our heads. Someone's finished *Daily News*

lies face down on the floor. The flood of sunlight
bending through the chrome-and-rubber

belly of the car becomes a priceless
Woolworth's angel, plays richly on her face.

The ticket-taker sways along the aisle, up
where the driver wishes himself gone.

*

All this frozen lattice work of sight and sound,
forgotten music, voice —
the midday city shaken

down to bare essentials —
shifting naked tree limbs,
cloudless urban glitter, ashen brims and shades.

Cuse Cuts

Through the recessed door of history, Saturday
high noon sunbeam dust and talcum powder,
hard autumn light, lime tile, the steel and leather
registers of service to the body — scattered

papers deck the low Formica tables, beneath
the amber holes of ashtrays — and above, a Zenith's
square gray face gets popped on for the games
at the far end of a broomhandle. In those days

vanished through the same retreating pinlight,
at first chill of winter in the legs, just whisked
off as a joke along with first ash at the temples —
all the athletes play injured, and well-known

aldermen walk up smartly for a midday haircut.
It's nothing much to interrupt the business
forecast with a sudden jolt — *You cut white hair,
don't you, Joe?* — that cracks the blinds and laughs

If you mean gray, of course. On screen, the manager
flashes signals. The junior partner removes
a comb and sharp set from the counter, pumps
the chair, and spins the seat to meet the man.

Ancient, Immaterial

The crude coin does not flatter
Julius Nepos, penultimate
ruler of the Western Empire.

On its head, the profile rises
in a rough smudge of pearled
hair, blank eyes, plunging nose,

the eternal smirk of privilege
and a weak long neck ready
for the blade. The reverse

holds a small cross undercut
by thorns and an overhanging
blast of olive branches, as if

pure gold could counteract
the poor workmanship, lack
of finish, and sleepy stagnant

effort made at the bankrupt
mint. The carelessness stuns
me—the hints, the slow drip

from pomp into irrelevance
as from a broken pipe into
hard clay. When did the holder

of this memento fling it back
over her shoulder into a ditch?
When did her faith give way

to the new reality, the separate
arrangement? The roar of dawn
that came when least desired,

night mysteries and ecstasies
all vanished, nothing left but
songs and lies, poems and pins

in the sky ready to wink out.
Not even the intrinsic value
in it mattered. The gesture

was required. Now, long after
almost every bit of the sad old
money has been smelted, buried,

or pierced and hung around
a mule's neck as a joke, the ghost
of its worth is blank under glass,

vanity on black velvet that I am
able to mock in the daylight, and
forbidden to touch at any price.

Grant in the Valleys

"The young have time to wait…"
~ *Donald Davidson, from "Lee in the Mountains" (1922)*

As disease emerges, rising through the face
like red veins of hematite, then whiteness,
and oceanic longing fills the eyes, the man's
already gone. I've seen it many times,
grown used to the progression. My regiment
was full of men who split like rotten boards
beneath the sun's saw blade at Cruces. When
the commanding officer clapped a hand on
my shoulder, grinned, and made me chief ward
of eighty cholera cases, assigned to me
a sortie into death, another look —
I was suddenly beneath contempt, just chaff,
a pile of horse grunt stacked five feet eight.
His expression deadened me. I can't forget
the tang of tropical hardwood burning long
into the night, huge moths and jungle scarabs
batting on the quiet tents where sick boys
witnessed the pooling of their short, bewildered
lives into a strange communion — to have come
this far for glory, to have exchanged the Gold
Rush for abrupt ruin in the rainy south,
barely aware of the leaf medicines and whiskey
we administered from oaken cups. All the time
gravediggers' picks worked on us from beyond
our meager perimeter of light. I swore an oath —
that if I survived the Isthmus, my mind intact,
I would thereafter prosecute my office
with a minimum of talk concerning honor,
my country, or my faithful service. I recognized,
somewhere in that sump of American desires,
in sole-worn boots and a greasy woolen tunic,
I was an instrument; my duty was to cut or rust.

*

On a bog-like San Francisco street that winter,
just off the Long Wharf promenade, the mist
from open water blurring the tinhorn crowd
in their shabby grog shops and faro parlors,
we stumbled on a knife-thrower at his game.
He had erected a fortune's wheel, with flags
that limply dangled from its outer edges.
In the center was a pretty dark-haired girl —
Sixteen? Black Irish? — she sat upon a stool
while the banners clicked and whirred behind
her — every nation of the world, it seemed.
We stepped closer. She wore a pink blindfold
and there was a tremble in her lower lip.
We saw that her legs shook beneath the satin
pantalettes she wore, and that her hands
somehow were pinned at her back. Not a few
in the crowd took special interest in this fact.
The man was stripped to the waist, his shoulders
steamed in the chill air and his bald pate shone
with perspiration. Turning from left to right,
testing his blades on strips of meat and cloth
not two feet from our faces, he made elaborate
display of the hardware. Then all at once, as if
a human pistol, he spun, and aimed, and flashed —
the knife whistled and struck Russia, buried to
its haft. The girl whimpered something softly,
then spoke louder. From one side came a laugh.
Around again, the pennants dropped and rose.
Both shuddering girl and mad marksman took
another turn. The sudden motion sprung,
she screamed in French, more laughter, this
time general, except for me. I'd missed again.
But the third time proved the charm. I've heard
that lost girl's declarations ever since —
I can't explain, these crowded memories
seem only loosely knit together — but she
comes back to me, an apparition from
the shallow grave of my first captaincy,

and not well-buried. Exactly this — the blade
sang, slowed in mid-air — I could not abstain —
and slammed into the flag of the United States.
"I love you! Love! I love!" she shrieked.
Then the pandemonium struck me dumb,
and I reeled back, and dropped a nearly full
Carpathian wineskin to empty in the street.

                              *

In those flush times, gold slugs fell like hail.
You couldn't find a backwoods trapper without
what should have been enough cash to buy
a Philharmonic, or found a Methodist college.
Cabbage, beets, and turnips sold at prices
high enough, you'd think your salads bronzed.
The world was full of desperate arrangements,
all fragile as spiders' webs in high wind.
Of course, like all, we thought ours ironclad.
In the long spare hours between morning drill
and turndown in the evening, we tended
potatoes — great rows of news and creamers.
We were going to light our cigars with dollars,
and shoe our horses with solid brass, once
that crop came in. But we weren't alone
in this brilliant notion, and by summer, when
the Columbia River gorged and did for us
what the fat market would have done, we laughed —
that's how fresh we were — afoot in clover,
enough biscuit and back bacon to feed that army
three times over. That food was speculation,
a running joke between us while we sipped
hot coffee and ate eggs. A time would come
when I'd see men carve shoulders from a beef
found bloated two days in a crossroads, and spit
shot from the pungent meat into the makeshift
cuspidor of a sun-bleached human skull.
I would see foul amputations dropped in wells

before the eyes of children, so their fathers
could not return and drink. The earth would give
abundantly, and I would reap the harvest —
everywhere, the circular stone crops of graves
requiring little sunlight, and no rain.

                              *

If I write the sour words some parlor hack
professors call a "memoir," you can bet
it will be at the bayonet point of poverty —
why else make a fool's rush into that land
of congratulations and confessions? Leave that
to priests and minor poets. Better to drift
off in unimpeachable silence — who knows
the true meaning of one's endeavors? Am I
a soldier first? A husband? A sublunary
pilgrim bound for better things? Are not
we all? Are you surprised that I believe?
I have not read this from a book, but I've
met Christ — though only once, and not for long.
On the lower Willamette, huddled husks
of the great coast tribes would come camp
near the stockade wall, trade pelts for trash
or firearms, and seek cures for the smallpox
that halved their number every year. For the most
part, we obliged — whiskey was good medicine,
and if it failed, a well-placed musket ball
would prove a true cure-all. It was here
that she appeared to me in the August haze,
bent with heavy grief, speaking fine English,
swimming in combinations of native skins
and Army issue clothes. Her husband had died
on the trail from Fort Vancouver, strength hissed
away by steam baths and worthless tinctures
purchased from the Hudson's Bay Company.
She hadn't a living relative left on earth,
and after a few weeks, a distance seemed

to gather in her bearing, like she was walking
through some other world, preferring that
to this. An unreal look of calm came on her —
something I could recognize, as I'd been
sometimes to that other place in spirits,
in that amber light of apprehension where
you can look in on yourself, and penetrate
the depths of Plato's cave, and see things as
they are, or as they seem to be, until
the spell is broken. She fixed me with a stare
that betokened all of this, and I was pulled
as if by gravity. More time elapsed.
At last, emboldened by several draughts
of cognac, I approached her at the camp.
Because of what my rank might represent,
she deigned speak to a half-drunk soldier.
In a wooded glade beyond the camp site,
we sat on an Army blanket and traded tales
for hours. In time, I fully came around —
you must know I'd heard none but brutal speech
for months, for years. For a long duration,
her words and mine were slow and natural
as branch water wending toward the ocean.
But then an unchaste music seemed to fill
my ears. I was on the verge of telling it —
the slant of light, the freedom of our talk,
the fullness of the life our bodies knew
for that one moment out of endless wars —
she must have seen before I had the chance.
She raised both hands and framed my face,
thumbs pressed gently at my temples. I saw
a sad tenderness I can't begin to fathom,
and she quoted me a verse I'd verify
years later — "The lamp of the body is the eye.
If the eye is good, your body will be full of light.
But if your eye is bad, your body will be
full of darkness. And if the light in you
is darkness, how very great that darkness is."

After she'd gone, I remained until the sun
went down, eyes levelling the same terrain
until it seemed I'd memorized each slope,
each subtle dip in the horizon, stretched
forth like an upturned palm. In latter days,
I learned to accurately read the land,
but there, all was mystery before me.
I had no premonition how her words
would come back on other, darker fields.

II

In the Republic of Tinnitus

Even rain falls at fifty decibels.
A screaming child revs the little
hammer to one hundred ten.

The odd shotgun blast or airbag
burst registers an irrevocable
one forty — not to mention

the takeoff of every Gibson
Flying V through heavy frost —
cones and circuits overloaded,

engineered for some tremendous
damage — fingers smashed on
unforgiving anvils, riven temples.

For me it's far past hopeless.
I've gorged too long on red level
chops and wine, sucked hard

on the corroded spigot where
the sonic acid flows. It's difficult
to even cut the grass without

lapsing into premature senility.
*Wear earplugs or earmuffs when
using power tools. Take precautions*

*at amusement parks and concerts.
Always remember to be conscious.*
Is that what Buddy Bolden said,

heels jammed in the rotten stirrups,
en route to joy and ruin through
the bell of his cornet on Canal Street?

Is that the dog or some ferocious
sounding member of the medical
establishment? I'll never know.

This nation's tricolor is ripped
almost in half. I live in outgrown
clothes. I slur my speech and drop

important documents into the fire.
The cannons have gone off and left
me deaf as an assistant principal

in the presence of a gamely truant.
It's all talk and strings, a singing
injury, at best a ghost sensation.

Sometimes there's kind of like
a ringing in my ears. That's all I have
to say about it. This is a free country.

Cigar Band Etiquette, 1987

This is a sin the British demand you redress,
bound to diminish even the best brands —
Bolivar, Cohiba, Montecristo, or Punch,
whatever the price or provenance, you risk
offense of your fellows if the paper ring stays
in its place a moment once the coal is fixed.

But the guilty drop of plant gum, affixed
by the rapid fingers of young girls dressed
for revolution, can tear the tender leaf — *It stays*
say some Americans, until the contraband
grows hot enough. So ignore the social risk,
and show off that Churchill with more punch.

Fidel Castro needs to have his ticket punched,
don't you think, Jim? The small stub was fixed
in his boss' lips. Every answer had its risks.
Well, there's something wrong with that battle dress
at his age. A bad joke, but at least he didn't brand
himself a bleeding heart. Lines of smoke strayed

into his drying eyes. The music came in staid
green and gold arrangements, as if punched
whole from 1940s broadcast swing. In this brand
of gathering, one looks for labels, easy fixes,
influential centers. One must carefully address
politics and God, or not at all. With less risk

involved, one had better dwell on this asterisk
to excess — pocket the cutters, purse the lips, stay
relatively safe and quiet, intent on window dressing.
Break these rules at your peril. To avoid a punch-
up with a drunk *aficionado*, don't fixate
on anyone's poise or handling. Lift the brandy

snifter slowly, and bring the glowing brand

to your mouth only out of doors, or else risk
poisoning the party. Whatever imprint's fixed
on your cigar, clutch it as if it were the mainstay
of your manhood. Be perceived as punctilious,
cosmopolitan, casual, cancerous, well-dressed.

In Cuba, the endless punched and branded bundles
addressed for the risky export market remain
key fixtures of a system stayed by other manners.

Grand Tour Weekend, 1997

We disembark on a slushed tarmac,
Calling on the New Sick Man of Europe's
Egg-crystal origins at the Hermitage;
We've come for the famous dead.

Calling on the New Sick Man of Europe's
Good graces, with a shovelful of cash
We've come for the famous dead.
The air is poor and there's a whine —

Good gracious! With a shovelful of cash
We can service all our vices, though
The heir is poor. And there's wine
At the guide's recommended hotel where

We can service all our vices, though
Our time is short. So we'll get drunk
At the guide's recommended hotel. *Where
in hell is the car we called from the air?*

Our time is short. *So?* We'll get drunk
on the favored exchange of the dollar
in hell. *Is the car we called from the air
one of those old Soviet jobs?* No one cracks.

On the favored exchange of the dollar
We disembark on a slushed tarmac —
One of those old Soviet jobs. No one cracks
Egg-crystal origins at the Hermitage.

Fluorescent Blues

Flash on and I become a white girl,
a pallid Weimar phantom, rose blooms
beneath my skin, phosphorescent face,
blown glass wrists and plastered locks —
spirits chilled under icy waves of light.

The function of the fluorescent bulb —
shine with striking flatness, destroy
whatever fragile skeins of conversation
connect you to me, us to them, reverse
utterly the religious campfire quietude
that once gave birth to gods, blast away
the blush of good dark wine, the soft
felt-headed hammers on piano strings,
the significant sparks of jewels — all these
chants too subtle for such electric fright.

A Cabinet Window

(after a print by Scott Stephens)

The sun's strong medicine
hinges far into midday —
little gods alive and dreaming
spirit light, sepal, leaf, and bloom.

Quiet cul-de-sac, solid brick face
at the foot of Cloverdale Drive —
a Zoloft shrine that glows
well into a baseless night.

Terra cotta, glass and lacquer
frame some daily gifts —
offices of ash and pine,
exploding pear and zoysia.

An unlocked moment
here before the stretch,
odd grimace, grin or sigh,
then soft pull of the latch.

Through the Chagall Windows

Hadassah-Hebrew University
Medical Center, Jerusalem

Shavings of twelve lives — the sons of Jacob
transformed first into the tribes, next made

over in the broken figures of dispersal — dry
leaves, smashed hands filigreed with dust.

This black wilderness of generations, all this
at last salvaged from the spectral lightlessness —

twelve refractions through twelve windows.
Creation in the arcing bright trajectories of birds

and in the blue fire of menorahs — preservation
in the vivid script of suns and oceans. New life

focused on the lantern of this city Synagogue,
itself walled otherwise by shards and surgeries.

Country of Stopped Clocks

Italo Calvino, 1923-1985

Cool mists on the cape jasmines never lift.
In another, faster world, gardenias — here

slow botanical breaths, light rain and surf,
fragrant tides, and laureled skiffs that top

the breakers, never reaching pristine shores.
No brambles in the terraced fields that skip

up the lush green hillsides — only row on
religious row of legumes, roots, and vines

to mark the buzz between monastic steps.
Honey bees at their cloudy mill work are

the only industry in this lazy country —
unfocused, massed to a lone vibrato note,

an elemental drone across the meadows.
I've consulted timetable, map and compass,

but the trains are thunderheads that mind
only their own low pressure, and the rails

ring nearby olive trees and orange groves,
by-passing cathedral, capital, and factory.

*

It was here, another time, we two together
traversed a vanished road, a string of cairns

to guide us through the stillness. Each mile
beneath the relentless, noon-locked sun

grew continental. We watered our horses
just beyond each ridge, wrote letters back

to civilization from every stand of oak,
brushed the dust, and made for the interior.

We never did arrive. One moment I was
sleeping, lost, or blind, and your sharp outline

raced ahead. I remember the glint of silver
set in the middle distance. I couldn't keep

apace as day stretched into day. The coast
came back beside me. The mourning doves,

stacked stones, and apple orchards — none just
as remembered — variations on a theme

that tumbles to a natural halt — as when
a blossom stops the hands, however fast.

Watchers Against Dawn

Time of dying wood smoke, ash and sky
the same gray spinal chill — eyes that dart
along horizons, that catch the first rose

fires burning down the hills — poor light
that breaks the dream, the night, the peace
where all is future, tense and untranspired.

The Turk sits on his cushion, prays his troops
will hold, polishes his blue scimitar, duly recites
his tattered battle lines. The Christian kneels

in his tent, palms his axe haft on the earth,
and prays the same dream in a different tongue.
The jockey moves through the slatted stable,

brushes his charger and hums an old tune
from the war. The pilot tightens her emerald
silks, slips on her leather against the cold

truth of the atmosphere, and squints into
the knife-like sun, now making itself known.
Steam pushes night up from the black lake

and the koi are stirred to swim. The skimmers
are aloft — the frogs' flat eyes in focus — the swan's
long neck uncurls. She shakes her lighted head

in water and begins. Close by, so many expectant
women and men close their eyes and press hands
over themselves, as they perfect loves not even

born, not even told in words. Their skins hold
more light than the rising day. And the single
bead of sweat or tear they shed alone is for

the moment a globe, in itself complete. When
the full light looms, when day's heat and commerce
have annihilated these small touches, killed them

even in memory, all these beings will accelerate
far past stopping into their wishes and instincts
and will contest some ground not half worth

having — toward dark quiet ends that can sustain
them only until tonight, tomorrow. So quiet,
the unlucky dead and the lucky dreaming,

so quiet, the hopeful populations of deep night.

Lazarus Road

So far from the bent nineteenth century
Alabama traces and the sweet rampant
vines of fog that curled those unforgiving

paths in-process — the idea of a journey
gone into action through the right whip
hand, fat red judge hanging in the sky.

Cobbles into crushed rock, lime dust
into lungs — a long coeval march until
the coffle disappears, one pair of hands

dissolved into another. Rain on this
hammer — I'll hand down to my brother
one more rusted instrument in time.

Gray bodies of the highway — ever-present
question marks and clover leaves, the past
behind and underneath half-fallen billboards,

signals of lost road diversions — matchstick
flares and burned-off fields for towering
on-screen kisses brighter than the moon.

Vast cities belted by a ten-lane tendency
to dream — all times at once, destinations
universal — expertly machined and faceless

integration of all parts — blowing paper,
wedding party, funeral cortege — all these
loose spirits most alive in constant motion.

"By the Banks of the Mighty..."

Belly down in bluestem grass, barely awake,
just alive to the hints of painted April,
headfirst on the swale, and gray beyond

belief — these bones can live. Such fine dust
compacts the dry shins and cracked
hips of the riverbed. Hard water ripped

along this ancestral pit twenty years ago,
shifted course, and shaved off part of Illinois
for Kentucky's blue moon commonwealth.

I lived through the flood. My father worked
a sandbag line twenty miles from Cairo. Away
three weeks, he wrote of how one Sunday

morning, a Baptist preacher led the whole
reeking mass through the Lord's Prayer, twice.
The heavens remained closed, and black mud

sucked at every boot, as if the ravenous earth
wouldn't wait to have them. And now it has
most everything, tucked safe beneath its skin —

hand-sewn shirt to home-made battle flag,
pipestone fragments to ruins of the gov't. pike,
sudden detonation of the coal oil stores,

burning barn, burning stable, burning prairie,
sad comfort in the upper room past midnight,
single lantern strung across the summer,

dark figures in the snow, at a great distance,
black pillar on the horizon, the one-time
show from Washington, shot to Springfield,

lilac garlands, new muscadine tipped back,
cross-ties joined, old growth oaks left alone,
high gold against gigantic tides of wind

— the ballast of two broad centuries, and those
two hundred springtimes, sifted into topsoil,
dreamed once in an acid flash, then consigned

to outer darkness. The flood year I turned
about to face my father, his unlikely path,
unbelievable straw hat and faded wash pants,

most of all to face his brotherhood, right
where rain and hail cut the states in half,
driven to our knees, and then to peace.

What if I'd been beside him then, in that
little grave behind the levee? It's where he
leaped and smiled, spade in hand, going on

to the immortal. He struck the ground
and spun it — dug in wrist-deep, whistling.
When they reached down to lift him out,

he'd seen ghosts in the country. Nothing
remains the same for long, I'm told. Take
this chord, this voice, this breathing body

sound asleep by the dry bank of a tired river.

Calamity's Blacktops

Summer-wide cascades of heat and light —
the stern dark mileage bowling through
frayed pasture land, ever-present empty

husks of snakes and insects, droning songs
at the hazy margins of the forest, the gentle
threats of fence wire at their given intervals —

a panoply of strong messages, set in motion —
scenes overtaking senses, place and time bent
into blazing aircooled union only at high speed.

On browning flat pans of the continent
where onslaughts of sun and rain punctuate
the long days with their headless arguments,

roads taken steam and hungry travelers suffer —
a jeep's rollbars wedge into a ditch, a sedan's
carjacked at the theme park — constant danger

at the crossings where no one completely stops.
But these roads have witnessed transient joys —
Roman candles, golden apple cores and condoms,

stray cash, paper flowers, flat harmonicas —
all figures of temporary fixes and the brilliant
cockamamie schemes hatched somewhere

far afield, along the way. Idling at the rest stops,
burning up the pavement, dreaming in the pink
opaque films of the horizon, all drivers make

their way from the bully boneyards of the past
deep into a calamitous west, its complicated
lanes overlapped, overcharged and ever-changing.

Rayon is Probably the Most
Misunderstood of All Fibers

Single-breasted, man-sized boxy cut of 1962,
zinc-lined container-cache of artificial silk,
woven of wood pulp — the whip-spun

fabric shines. San Diego, Saigon, Omaha —
the epoxies are fixing under black lamps.
Prototypes of plastic rifles are misfired

in the hands of new recruits. Breathing hoses
come unconnected in the stratosphere
while static clogs the single artery to Moscow.

Tissue death ensues in thirteen seconds.
Tick. Tick. Tick. Grandfather's tuxedoed
legacy unsentimentally changes hands

in s.o.b. Harry Delaney's Thrift and Pawn
at the low rent terminus of Sixth and Grand.
Make way for the slick black coat the War

made possible — no cheap knock-off from Japan.
Notice the hang of the slacks, the precision
seams and clever stitching. Not a wasted

motion through the blinding yellow aperture
down into the basement bar and chop house
where matching jackets are suffused with light —

gel reds and copacetic blues, lighting into "Moody's
Mood for Love" — the sunken evening is reduced
to prime. And at table two, elbows cocked

at frozen angles, chin in hands and swizzle sticks
fanned out in apprehension of the missile crisis,
a company man goes through his piss-poor motions —

sips his drink, rehearses facts, links raw files
to the fibers on his person — true / false, *note switches'*
off or on position, single / married, *have you now or have*

you ever, alive / deceased, *please indicate your faith*
preference in the blank, female / male, *purely for*
recordkeeping purposes—a battery of the MMPI

duly noted in the minutes. Such roomy sleeves.
Impervious to moths or silverfish. A fashion
trend far past revival. But on the pressing

tables of the day, by the burning finish of the '60s,
inflammable rayon stands apart from cotton,
linen, nylon, polyester. The decade's thread

becomes unstable and may shrink when wet.
In every case, avoid wringing excess moisture
from the garment. Smooth and shape, dry flat.

Light like Palm Springs

*"Okay baby, I'll get out. You can find me in
Palm Springs. I'll be there..."*
~Frank Sinatra to Ava Gardner, 1952

This cement mirage, this teal and aquamarine
monument, this mountainous bonfire, perfect

simulation of an oasis, a blue-flame basis
of cool dreams, apart from all the gruesome

greens and blacks of valley lands that flood
and parch according to the seasons. Here

our air is dry, but we can dreamily dip into
the chlorinated ocean and gaze at those majestic

legs that gleam poolside through coal-colored
goggles, our hearts and bellies sunk beneath

the waterline. A town that flickers like summer
light on waves, a pure pipe dream, it's whatever

in the dictionary is the opposite of Hoboken —
which brings Sinatra himself inevitably into this

picture, along with all his trappings. He's set
sail on extraordinary renditions of the martini —

clear gin seas and vermouth mists, and so bobs
from the corner booth through swinging doors,

drops the growling Pontiac into drive and plants
a flat foot on the gas. He tightens his tie, ties

his shoelaces, buys a velvety box of chocolates
on Palm Canyon Drive and dumps them in the tub

where she's under bubbles in a champagne rage.
Oh baby wouldya can the naked aggression already?

This and other roles from acting lessons. They box
their shadows, dancing, landing rabbit punches —

I know all too well EXACTLY who "you" are.
Cigarette stubbed, water slapped, and then arms limp.

*My mother told me to expect this. I should have
known* — and all the other dirty laughs we love

them for. The camera slowly pans away and left.
Bruise-black darkness saturates the screen and then

it's ours — the dream of desert light, the good joke
and the getaway, the thick T-bone and the deep wine,

the pills for play and staying power, the moony
curves of floor-length gowns and the shine from

silk fedoras. Most of all — our fortunate distance
from the past, and our luck not to have to live it.

The Painted Men

A million mottos for the stretched canvas of a bicep,
pipe-like forearm, pectoral plain, or shoulder blade —
five seconds of uneasy smiles as the meat in question
settles and the needle whirs to speed. In the moment

when whatever boyish dream is permanently muscled
into our bodies, and the pain-shock spikes its scripture
home, rosettes of blood rise in the shape of some idea —
any military death's head, delicious cartoon succubus,

cool motorcycle ape, or logocentric badge of chaos is just
our pin-prick toughness, a distraction, a substitute for soul
below the skin, above the bones. Once we were good
at rousing fear in youth pastors and old ladies. These days

even the Army will take our green sleeves gladly, sign
our shining crosses and our barbed-wire bleeding hearts
to a commitment even greater than the ones we chose
as we trolled the books and posters for a message

meant to last. What has driven us, brothers of the wild
Occident, to this meth lab burlesque of tribal medicine?
Our walkabouts are conducted on well-policed streets;
our TV dreamtime's damaged; our sweat lodge has been

flea-bombed and sprayed with disinfectants. In the great
gambling halls of national politics, our protests fall silent
as the tongue and lips logo, scribbled yin-yang, L-O-V-E
and H-A-T-E, Semper Fi, Wino Forever, sunglassed dogface.

No Van-Dyked Devil has to grin and wink to demonstrate
our critical lack of foresight. Next morning, our buddies
made us do it, or maybe it was the booze. We button
shirts over our comic courage and get right back to work.

A Cutting

Voice of an exhausted angel
frayed at the high end, piano-
backed and soft in her dark room.

Claustrophobic bed-length blue
notes catch each falling drop.
By candlelight, all her poems

scalloped on the floorboards—
Love what will and will not do
in gothic calligraphic curls.

Locks and buckles tight across
this space reserved for her,
the always-crouching figure

who listens for another voice
to demonstrate what love is—
not some bleak joke, a message

novel as a glass of chocolate milk.
And she in a more than unclothed
condition, shadowed on the wall.

One way to comprehend herself,
nerve sparks to ragged ends,
is to touch the separations

of her skin to open air, the tool
to its translation. A tearless
murmuring of love-words,

spoken as she crouches still,
falling from the glistening lip
alone, precise as poems.

Her history in purple
marks made across her arms,
misery of springs where

womanhood comes looking
for her, turns, and runs
so far from this Van Nuys

split-level that no one
will even recognize what
she looks like in ten years.

And for now, the small gains
of adderall and ugly gossip
countered here, in quiet

contemplation of an art form,
dabbling by the bridge
no one comes back over —

you know — an ice compress
by her side, a roll of gauze,
the razor steady cuts all clean —

so much desire for it now —
the shadow motion's smooth
long lines, the dappled pages.

The Monk Stripped Bare by His Brethren, Even

It's the birthday of Marcel Duchamp
and money's draining from the maple trees

in a modernistic copper flourish, saying
something — "Well, You Needn't" — dripping

down on soft chinchilla cuffs that ring
the hands of some rare beauty. A garish

plum and alabaster face now comes close
to whisper her requests. Half a pace

behind, the bursar with his sudden double
rolls and books is pocketing the change.

A Reel of "Miners' Lifeguard"

Dead midnight of the 19th Century —
dark ropes of profuse veins beneath

the skin just waiting to be burned.
A deforested and cross-tied section

where the right-of-way has grown
up to this bully scene of progress

seeding deaths in all directions —
yellowed grass on land and floating fish

across the mercurial sheen of lakes,
taste of sulphur from the deeper wells.

To score this landscape, banjo music —
huck-a-backs to wipe the beaten down,

canned hash to build them up again —
and all the paunchy chuffer headmen

tipping every balance their own ways.
The unknowns ganging to be cheated,

lining single-file behind corroded pushcarts —
faces that vanish every twelve-hour day.

Rounds of small beer under stars.
The smooth contingencies of theft get

mentioned far into the morning. *Keep your hand
upon that dollar and your eyes*

upon that scale. Some agitated blade demonstrates
the proper way to build a bomb —

head-first. Someone kicks his heels up
laughing, someone cuts an Irish jig and reel.

Versus Physiognomy's Prophets

Jack Johnson 1878-1946

Their faces radiate every necessary move —
good and evil shine together in their eyes,
in their chins and fragile jaw lines always
their certainties arise, Bible truths re-read

within the ring. How many primer lessons
in destruction are needed until these fools
learn a house burns hottest from its center,
its blazes radiating outward finally to lick

the cold night sky? Gold, white and blue trade
space above the fairgrounds as we toil and spin.
These opponents chuff and lumber toward me,
furious and mulish in their movements,

mush-mouthed, blond, ignorant as timber.
Fast or slow, this deft footwork baffles them.
In floods from arctic lakes, I pour it on —
Do something! Let me see what else you've got!

As they fume and stumble, a new arrangement
becomes plain. And I'll swing in left and right
to telegraph the bulletin worldwide. So after
the modest interval that decency demands,

after the sun passes its high point and burns
the tight faces of this cigar-chewing crowd,
after the liars' proclamations have all but gone
up in the next days' papers, I close distance,

nearer than a friend. For an instant, we dream
the fight is finished, and all sounds diminished
except the ever-crackling fires of this world.
I watch from a distance as my right arm heaves

back and shatters him. Next thing, he's a fish
flapping on the canvas, and bad fortune groans
from below. It's within these ice-bound spaces
between rage and realism that I must contend.

And yet it's so dim beneath this dented moon.

"Reminiscing in Tempo"

"If you like the music, tell all your friends. If
you don't like the music, don't tell nobody."
~Bob French, WWOZ 90.7 FM New Orleans

It used to be that the signal
would emerge for us, road-bound
and thirsty, only like a sudden

cloudburst over the causeway.
You can't forget the shock —
the knockout cuts that dropped

one after another, imperiously
flipped and framed in the way
only master DJ's do. *You know,*

these boys got to get back to that
kind of record — meaning Art &
Aaron Neville. A dissertation

on the superior state of Jazz
Fest *circa 1975 — a little too much*
Lenny Kravitz is what's the problem

today. Not that I have anything
against him. Such rare and fleeting
pleasures in the skips and pops,

the long-buried jewels served
from 45s in that pistol-hot time
signature, the just-hung together

Hammond organ and the over-
loaded tube amp blues endemic
to the city's heart and soul — even

the misattributed tunes, the lost
search for misremembered sides,
the yawning presence of dead air,

even these communicated a full-
time love, freely volunteered,
self-realized, not part of some slick

corporation's program concept —
spongy song-filler for so many
antiperspirant cans. Not once

you crossed the bridge to 'OZ.
It could be any hour, from dawn
to well past midnight — sweetness

broadcast from the little closet
studios tucked into a disused
corner of the park near Congo

Square. All day long the boom
mikes were open, turntables spun,
smoke rose and unseen hands

enacted dramas of the past.
You would tumble insouciantly
from cars and taverns, taking

that companionship for granted,
at last letting it dissolve and hiss
into flatlining noise back north

above Slidell. Those were the days
before the waves were digitized,
the local music calendar blown up

large for all the world. How can I
play the surly purist hard enough
to turn my back on progress?

I turn to it, point to it, motion
toward the great station and its
memories, import a sentimental

fraction of it to my present life,
send my check and get the sticker
in return. But some few mornings,

the glory of its ghost returns,
just a flutter and I can fall down
to the business of recording.

A Case for Pluto

Third cold of the winter — and while
you tumble through it with a sniffle,
tonight after you return to mama's

I'll scorch this beast with codeine
and will be laid out for three days.
There's no other way to do it now

that my body and I have agreed
to finally stop fucking around
with each other — you may get it

when you're forty. There are worse
things in the world. Like this one —
last night I saw plain evidence

that our system was diminished.
There in outer space, our favorite
cartoon cat and his little kid friends

were on a bubble cruise from point
A to Z around the planets, and right
past the icy rainbow rings of Saturn,

and the blue twins Uranus and Neptune,
the game just stopped. *Now that we've*
visited all eight, let's zoom whoom on

back home! Zing a ma doodle! Damn.
It had hit us at last, this astro-travesty
I've watched unfold without a peep

for years, first in *The New York Times,*
then vaguely on some sleepy science
TV show, and at last in bored bar talk

with some geeky friends. But it wasn't
real until last night. I thought they'd
dropped it and moved on to better things.

But no, that never happens. And so
it came home in a cloud of pixels when
you learned there were a mere eight

planets in our solar system, and (thank
you Jesus) we (still) lived on the third.
I couldn't believe it at the time and barked

That's wrong — they forgot Pluto! Not
knowing what you'd think. *What's Pluto?*
And for my life I couldn't answer you

completely straight. *Well, a planet. It used
to be a planet, but they thought it was too
small* — no idea if that was right, like so

many other instant bits of wisdom since
your birth. *We should tell the scientists,*
you said. *We should!* I sneezed. *Are you*

ok, Daddy? Then I put the dishrag down.
Of course I am. Don't worry. And the show
went on just like it should. The goofy cat

continued as we knew he would, with
a honk and a laugh, then back to the dream
world where he lives, not all that

far from here. My cold will go, spring
is close, and you will learn to ride
a bike, to swim, and to write a loopy

sentence in a year or two. Whatever
happens with us, whatever they say,
we'll look up and know that the planet

Pluto is out there somewhere, just
a little giggle wobble on its orbit through
our common sky, on the cool side of the sun.

White Hours

Play begins at noon, beneath
the ocean's depthless clouds —
high crowns of early summer.

Difficult access to a telescoping
dream — candy striped umbrellas,
foam footballs, semi-conscious

readers drifting to another shore,
tall Cokes pulled from the cold,
rib racks grilled under the sun.

If I could have remained still,
peering at the whitecap lines,
at peace below the arcing gulls,

someone might have taken me
for a reflective man, dressed well
in the oven of his own red skin.

But you know I love to move,
to talk, to stir, to sweat, to smash
anything into the steady metal

machine of time, make it confess
its inhuman plan to burn and curl
each one of our white hours to ash.

Given that, will you forgive my tricks
with cards, offhand tickling games,
and the clatter of my idle words?

I hear some muted minor chords.
I'm trained to undercut the tempo,
to slow and speed the gorgeous hillside

above the resolution of an English
abbey — so far removed, the light
alone remains, across the hemispheres.

In this stolen stretch, this beach
walk lifted from that receding day,
now lowered into this bookstore,

stateroom, wedding chamber,
this acolytes' enclosure where
we're gathered, love, with friends,

I can see the red and gold parasail
open over the gulf, feel the sand
give beneath my feet, and finding

the horizon, note the passage made
miles into the present with you,
my traveler, alive and keeping time.

Mel Bay Beginning Guitar Method,
Kool Keith, and Me

He looked to be a calloused old jump-jazzer,
or a preternatural five string picker sprung
from the bosom of the Ozarks — patient,
anaesthetic grin in every frame, same cream
jacket, narrow black stripe tie, Brylcreem
shine and hands cradled around that blonde
hollow body — art deco machine heads, pearl
inlays, and a single nickel pickup — the man
had tone to spare. You could sense it even
in the sound-proofed, grainy black and white
practice rooms of Guitar Fun, Inc., tucked behind
the utopian rows of white Les Pauls, the sinister
SGs decked in black and red, the dulcet Strats,
the working stiff Teles in humble woodgrain, even,
in memory, the godfather's austere Hofner Bass —
the whole trophy room abuzz with an electric
glamour, at a level of expense and exposure
my mother was not willing to abide. So on
Christmas morning I tumbled down the stairs
to find a sarcophagic Washburn acoustic guitar
laid beneath the tree, shrouded in a beige plastic
zip-up cover, steel strings bright for the blood
of my soft fingers — a perfectly fine instrument
that I couldn't make sound right, no matter
at what angle I cocked my little hips and bluffed
those greasy chords. What I did accomplish,
thanks to Mel Bay's book, was a brain-leveling
range of "Tenting To-nights" and "Aura Lees" —
ping-ping-ka-ping, ping-ping-ka-pong, ping-ping-ka-pung.
It would have been a total loss if it wasn't for
Kool Keith. He wasn't who you think. He was
my first and only teacher of guitar, who every
Tuesday from four until five-thirty descended
from the Lake Street El, and from the West Side
clubs, and from an existence I could only peek at

from the school bus and the liner notes, to suffer
through my tinsel trick beginning method skills.
Each week, he'd blow through the front doors,
smile at my mother and the man who made this
deal for him. There would be a minute's talk
about the rise and fall of some engagement, a hot
set just played, or heard, or out on vinyl, sometimes
the grinning backbites about some other local player,
then he'd stoop to me and laugh — *All ready? You
practice hard this week?* Automatic, but I would be
impressed. The natty double-breasted leather,
the tight Afro, down just low enough for '79,
the black wingtips, and most of all the sunburst
Ibanez slung at his side, ensconced in its battered
hard body road case, stickers reading like some
hieroglyphs — Ampeg, Zildjian, D'addario — what
in the name of God could all that mean? To me,
it was a parti-colored index to the Kool. When Keith
would settle in his metal folding chair, light his
Camel, and flip the clips, the weeklong lid was off
of a true mystery, and the pink plush inside of it
was visible even to me. He'd plug in with a pop,
and tune up with what looked like radar while I blew
on a pitch pipe. As my weak notes ran all together,
and my chords dropped dead against the frets,
Keith would look far off, past the sheets, and smoke
somewhere on his own. Half the time I'd dribble
my pick into the sound hole, and Keith would
have to root around in his case on my behalf.
I wouldn't lose those hard-earned prizes — heavy,
marbled green and black — I couldn't believe
that I could keep them. His turn, and I would
wonder at the sudden life in those shitty little songs —
amp'ed, sped or slowed, phased or clean, fed-back
in colors I couldn't comprehend. He had these
t-shirts, one black, a mock-up of the golden
arches, *Marijuana*. Another, red, *Enjoy Cocaine*.
These were words I'd heard in vague reference

to John Lennon, who had gone into retirement
because of *Rx* (drugs) — and I understood that drugs
meant jail or brain damage. But not Kool Keith.
He wouldn't do that to me. I was his biggest fan.
At the blessed early end of a lesson, once,
he looked into the slush of Ridgeland Avenue
and realized there wasn't any rush. I sat hunched
over the instrument I would quit in six months
to go back to bats and tennis rackets, small hands
clamped around the lawless neck, elbows hinged
over the lacerated pickguard and punched-up body.
He was thoughtful enough to ask me about my math
grades. My math grades. When I'd finished mumbling,
he drew a deep breath and asked, asked me, *Mind*
if I just play? And then he practiced riffs I had no
idea existed. He turned a knob and tore off a blues
I'd never heard in person. He smiled at my dazzled
look and then ran up another flag. This time he
wandered into something deep, and, turning, hit
a vein of silver. His eyes were closed and two strong
lines of smoke piped from his nostrils. I tried
to listen and was left far behind, chewing gum, certain
just of this — the world was greater than I'd thought.

www.ingramcontent.com/pod-product-compliance
Lightning Source LLC
Chambersburg PA
CBHW022037090426
42741CB00007B/1099